Jesus Lives!
The Easter Story

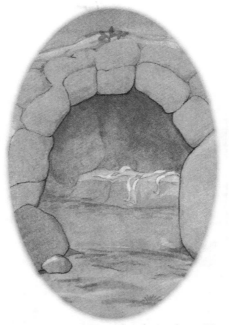

retold by
LAURA DERICO

illustrated by
RONDA KRUM

"He is not here; he has risen!"
from Luke 24:6

Story based on Matthew 21–28; Mark 14–16; Luke 22–24; and John 13–21.

© 1999 Standard Publishing, Cincinnati, Ohio. A division of Standex International Corporation.
Sprout logo and trade dress are trademarks of Standard Publishing.
Printed in the United States of America.
Cover design by Robert Glover.

Library of Congress Catalog Card Number 98-61299
ISBN 0-7847-0892-4

08 07 06 05 04 03 02   9 8 7 6 5 4 3

Standard
PUBLISHING
CINCINNATI, OHIO

The King is coming!" the people shouted.
A large crowd gathered to see Jesus.

Soon Jesus came into the city of Jerusalem, riding on a young donkey.

"Hosanna in the highest!" the people shouted to Jesus. "Blessed is he who comes in the name of the Lord!"

Jesus and his disciples went to the upper room of a house in the city to celebrate Passover together. As the meal was being served, Jesus wrapped a towel around his waist.

He took a bowl of water and began washing the feet of all of his disciples. When he was finished, Jesus said, "Follow my example. You should serve others just as I serve you."

During the meal, Jesus reminded the disciples that he would soon leave them. He took bread, gave thanks to God, broke it, and gave it to his disciples. He also took the cup, gave thanks, and gave it to his disciples.

Jesus said, "I'm giving this bread and cup to you. Remember me whenever you eat bread and drink from the cup together."

When they had finished the meal, they sang a song of worship to God and went to the Mount of Olives.

Jesus and his disciples went to a garden to pray.
Jesus took Peter, James, and John with him and said,
"My heart is heavy because I am so sad. Stay here
with me."

Then Jesus went a little farther by himself and prayed to God, "Father, I will do whatever you want me to do."

Jesus prayed this prayer three times. Each time, he went back and found his disciples sleeping, because they were very tired. The third time, Jesus woke them, saying, "Let's go! The one who will betray me is here!"

Judas Iscariot had been one of Jesus' friends. But now he came with men to arrest Jesus.

They took Jesus to the high priest to be judged. Some people were angry that Jesus said he was the Son of God. They didn't believe Jesus, even though he only spoke the truth.

No one could find anything bad that Jesus had done. Even the governor, Pilate, wanted to set him free. But the crowds shouted, "Crucify him!" So Pilate turned Jesus over to the soldiers to be crucified.

Jesus was quiet. He knew this was part of his Father's plan.

The soldiers took Jesus away. They dressed him like a king, with a purple robe and a crown of thorns. They made fun of Jesus. They did not understand that the kingdom Jesus talked about was not like earthly kingdoms. It was the kingdom of God!

They led Jesus to a place called Calvary. There they crucified him with two criminals, one on his right and one on his left.

But Jesus still loved the people. From the cross, he said, "Father, forgive them. They do not know what they are doing."

Darkness came over the whole land. With his last breath, Jesus cried out, "Father, I put myself in your hands!" Then he died.

The earth shook and rocks split. The men who were guarding Jesus said, "He really was the Son of God!"

A rich man named Joseph was a follower of Jesus. He asked Pilate for Jesus' body so he could bury him. He placed Jesus' body in a new tomb and rolled a big stone in front of the entrance.

Some of the leaders of the people were afraid that Jesus' friends would come to take his body out of the tomb. So Pilate sent guards to the tomb to seal it and watch it.

At dawn on the first day of the week, Mary Magdalene and some women went to the tomb. They wanted to put spices on Jesus' body, as was the custom of their people.

But when the women arrived at the tomb, they were amazed! An angel of God had rolled the stone away and was sitting there. He was bright like a lightning flash and his clothes were as white as snow.

The angel said to the women, "Do not be afraid. Jesus is not here. He has risen, just as he said. Jesus lives!"

The women were so happy that they ran to tell all Jesus' disciples. The disciples were amazed. Could Jesus really be alive?

YES! JESUS LIVES!

Jesus appeared to the women and to his other disciples many times. He wanted to show them that he was alive so they could tell others.

He told them, "Go and tell all nations about me. Baptize them in the name of the Father, Son, and Holy Spirit. Teach them to obey everything I have told you. I promise that I will always be with you."

The disciples believed Jesus and did what he said. They were filled with joy, knowing that . . .

JESUS LIVES!